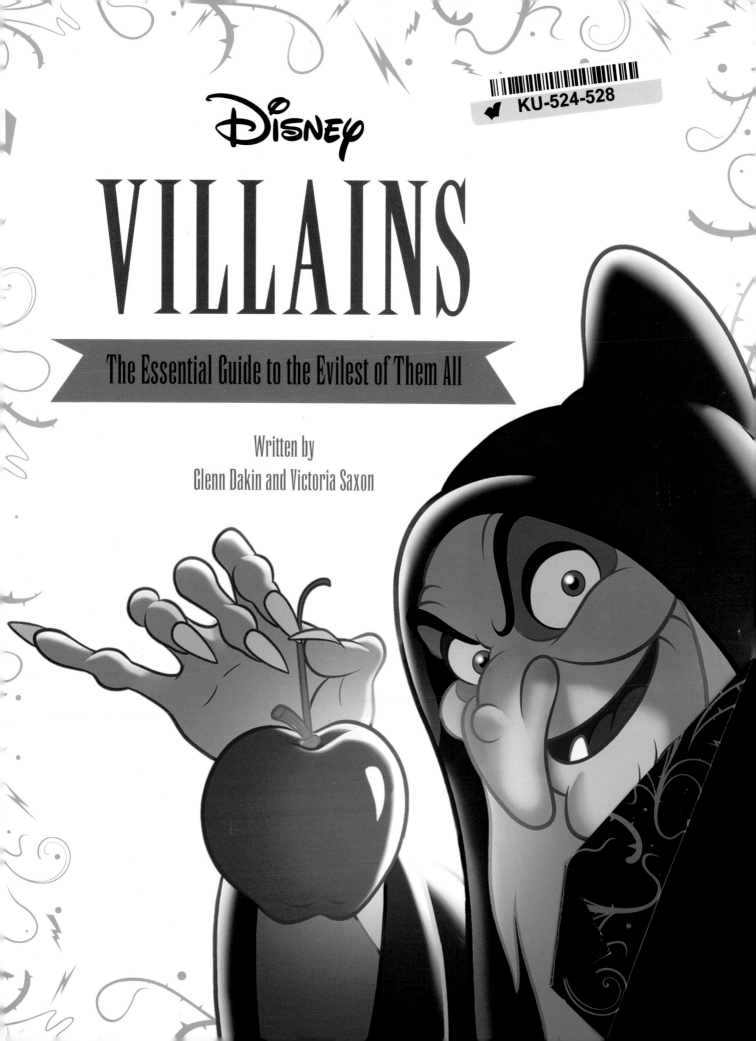

KU-524-528

DISNEP

VILLAINS

The Essential Guide to the Evilest of Them All

Written by
Glenn Dakin and Victoria Saxon

Contents

Introduction

Are you the kind of person who detests happy endings? Does it make you sick to your stomach when the fair princess marries her charming prince? Does it boil your blood to see a hero defeat a villain and make him look silly in the process? No? Well, thank goodness! That means you're not as bad as the scoundrels in this book! Prepare to be scared out of your wits by the dastardly deeds of the vilest villains you could ever loathe to meet. You're going to love hating every single one of these sinister stinkers!

Ursula

Two-faced and terribly tricky, Ursula is an incredibly powerful sea witch. Part mermaid and part octopus, this tentacled terror casts spells with the worst of intentions. She sees Ariel's love for Prince Eric as her chance to gain what she wants the most – total control of the sea!

Nails painted in her signature red

⭐ Banished

This sorceress was once a favourite at the court of Triton, king of the sea. However, she was banished from Atlantica long ago and sent into exile.

About Ursula

⚡ Ursula is very vain. She thinks she is so powerful, nothing can stop her.

⚡ She says she will help Ariel, but she plans to steal her soul and her voice.

⚡ Don't trust anything she says... there's always a catch!

Now I am the ruler of all the ocean!

Jetsam is Flotsam's twin and constant companion

She has only six tentacles

★ Power hungry

Ursula has always held a grudge against Ariel's father, King Triton. She is determined to get her revenge and overthrow him.

King Triton barters his own soul to save Ariel. This makes Ursula queen of the sea!

★ In disguise

To prevent Ariel from marrying the man of her dreams, irksome Ursula disguises herself as "Vanessa" and tries to tempt Prince Eric to the altar.

Ursula might change her face, but she can't hide her bad attitude for long.

11

Underwater Lair

Exiled from the sea kingdom, and with her wicked mind seething with plans for revenge, Ursula is forced to find a secret place to hide away. In the darkest, creepiest trench in the ocean, she discovers a terrifying skeleton and calls it home.

⭐ Dragon's den

Ursula's lair is built within the rotting remains of an extinct dragonfish. She spirited away a few tons of rotting flesh (rumour has it she actually ate them!)

Ursula's "little poopsies", Flotsam and Jetsam, lure Ariel back to the sea witch's dark domain.

Fanged entrance hall

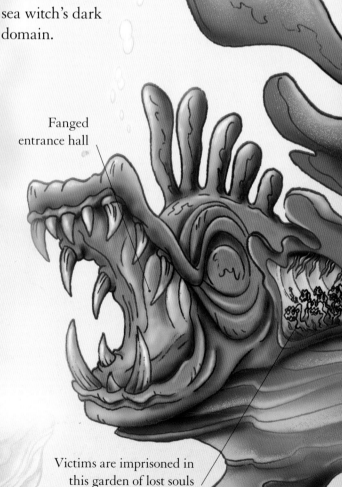

Ursula has powerful magic, and she loves to use it on her foes. Poisonous potions are her speciality.

Victims are imprisoned in this garden of lost souls

Dragonfish
skeleton

Giant shell
lounger

⭐ Shipwrecked

Growing to a massive size, Ursula prepares to
destroy all her foes with the power of Triton's
trident. But Prince Eric sails a wrecked ship
straight at her, piercing her bloated body.

Ursula towers over everything
and everyone. Yet her vast size
is also her downfall.

The stormy seas swallow
Ursula's body, and soon she
is just another dish for the
hungry little fish to dine on.

Crystal ball beams
images to Ursula from
Flotsam and Jetsam

Vanity table
and mirror

13

Dark Desires

I want to be dirty, filthy, stinking rich!

Some villains have their hearts set on silly things, like wanting someone else's pretty dress. Others desire something bigger, such as wanting to rule the kingdom! They soon learn they should be careful what they wish for!

Dark-haired Drizella

Red-haired Anastasia

 ## Anastasia and Drizella
CINDERELLA

The only thing this pampered pair care about is marrying someone rich and important. The nasty sisters are selfish and cruel to their stepsister, Cinderella, and they do all they can to make her life miserable. It's quite a shock for them when Prince Charming falls in love with Cinderella!

The lazy sisters have been spoiled by their mother, Lady Tremaine.

Beautiful dresses all carefully cleaned by Cinderella

Skull brooch holds
his robes in place

Fiery blue
hair turns
red in anger

*It's a small
Underworld
after all, huh?*

Hades
HERCULES

Hot-headed Hades is painfully
jealous of his brother Zeus,
king of the gods. This bad-
tempered brute hates the
Underworld and the other gods
on Mount Olympus so much
and wants nothing more than
to steal the throne for himself.

Hades' anger makes his blue-flamed
hair turn red-hot.

Pointy horns rip
through robe

The Horned King
THE BLACK CAULDRON

The Horned King wants to
find the Black Cauldron so he
can rule the army of the dead.
He controls many evil forces,
but he has no magic powers.
He kidnaps a magical pig
named Hen Wen, to use
her powers instead. In the
end, he is destroyed by the
Black Cauldron itself!

*Arise, my messengers
of death!*

15

Jafar

Greedy and power hungry, Jafar is a sorcerer who is second in command to the Sultan of Agrabah. As a trusted advisor, he is powerful, but Jafar hates being second best. This sneaky snake hopes to capture the magic lamp so that he can take the Sultan's job and rule the whole kingdom.

The Sultan's daughter

Jasmine can see right through Jafar. She does not trust him and simply refuses to give him the respect he craves. She certainly does not want to ever be his wife!

Not worthy

Jafar has spent a lifetime searching for the Cave of Wonders. He is desperate to get his hands on the magic lamp that lies inside. However, he is far too afraid to go in himself.

The Cave of Wonders is filled with treasure, but it will swallow up anyone who is not worthy.

I'm just getting warmed up.

Jafar uses his evil powers to hypnotise the bumbling Sultan.

Big mistake

When Jafar finally gets his hands on the magic lamp, his bid for world domination doesn't go to plan. He wishes to be a genie, accidentally trapping himself inside the magical lamp!

Completely bald head hidden under his hat

Jafar couldn't bear to be less powerful than a genie, but he forgot about the itty bitty living space!

Staff with the head of a snake

About Jafar

↯ Jafar is the royal vizier of Agrabah.

↯ He has evil powers of sorcery.

↯ Jafar can hypnotise the Sultan to get him to do whatever he wants.

Jafar's parrot, Iago, is a talkative companion

Bad Bullies

These mean villains don't fight fair. They use superior physical strength, money, or power to bully smaller, weaker characters. It gives them such an advantage over their victims that they're almost impossible to beat.

High purple collar

Green gem in ring matches earrings and brooch

Grimace reflects his constant unhappiness

Lyle T. Rourke
ATLANTIS: THE LOST EMPIRE

Lyle T. Rourke has physical strength as well as power from his military position. He uses both to bully those around him. He even threatens to hurt the poor king of Atlantis, who is an old and sickly man.

I love it when I win!

Lady Tremaine
CINDERELLA

This wicked stepmother envies Cinderella's charm and beauty. Cruel and conniving, she makes poor Cinderella a servant in her own home. Lady Tremaine may not hurt Cinderella physically, but with her cruelty she causes her stepdaughter so much pain.

Big Bad Wolf
THE THREE LITTLE PIGS

The Big Bad Wolf's only goal is to eat the Three Little Pigs. He is ruthless and is always plotting a way to capture them. He often uses disguises to trick them. The Wolf may be stronger and taller than the pigs – but luckily he is also not nearly as clever!

Braces hold up baggy trousers

Mouth waters at the thought of eating pigs

Sailor's hat

Large, looming physique

I'm gonna knock you right into next week!

Pete
MICKEY MOUSE AND FRIENDS

Pete is always trying to hurt poor Mickey Mouse. He's a lot bigger and stronger than Mickey, and he spends a lot of time bullying him. As Mickey's boss and rival for Minnie Mouse's affections, Pete is just plain mean.

19

Maleficent

Maleficent is the most powerful and evil of all the fairies. Indeed, she even calls herself "the mistress of all evil". This vile-tempered fairy is filled with fury when she is left out of the celebrations for the new princess Aurora's birth. An angry Maleficent is a scary sight – and upsetting her is a big mistake!

Uninvited guest

This cruel fairy shows up uninvited to Princess Aurora's christening and casts a spell on the tiny princess. The curse states that Aurora will die on her 16th birthday!

Maleficent curses Aurora to prick her finger on a spinning wheel and die.

Revenge

Three good fairies, Flora, Fauna, and Merryweather, keep Aurora hidden from Maleficent for 16 years. Finally, Maleficent finds the princess on her birthday!

Maleficent commands Aurora to touch the spindle. The cursed princess does as she is told.

Horned
headdress

Pet
raven

Glowing
orb tops
her magical
scepter

Long black
robes with
purple
lining

About Maleficent

- She lives in a castle at the top of the Forbidden Mountain.
- She is very proud and demands respect.
- She has a short temper and flies into a rage easily.

You poor simple fools, thinking you could defeat me!

The goons

Maleficent has an army of bumbling fools who carry out her wishes. They wear black armour and come in all shapes and sizes. Although fiercely loyal, they are not very good at their jobs.

Maleficent's silly goons waste years looking for a baby instead of a growing girl.

Forbidden Mountain

Towering over Forbidden Mountain is a fortress bristling with needle-sharp towers, draped with grotesque gargoyles. From here, Maleficent launches the search for Aurora. She is determined to make sure her curse comes true. Little does she know, the curse has already been weakened.

 ## Sleeping princess

Aurora does not die after pricking her finger. Instead, she falls into a deep sleep. Only Prince Phillip can awaken her with his kiss. The vile villainess tries to stop him with every dirty trick in the (spell) book!

Maleficent masterminds the search for Aurora from the highest tower.

Prince Phillip battles through a ring of thorns with his Sword of Truth.

Maleficent did not think about the power of good magic over evil, or the strength of true love! In the form of a dragon, Maleficent battles Prince Phillip. Punctured by the prince's sword, Maleficent falls into a fiery pit.

Maleficent changes into a fire-breathing dragon to fight Prince Phillip.

Wings to fly over rooftops

Flames shoot from the dragon's mouth

Can whip victims with sharp tail

Power Hungry

Hair flips when he dances

Red sash worn for a royal occasion

These villains can put on a good show. They may seem like true friends or advisors, but really they just love being close to royalty or power. And watch out for the ones who are only trying to gain more control for themselves!

Duke of Weselton
FROZEN

This arrogant duke loves money and power. He goes to Elsa's coronation to try to weasel the best trade deal for himself. However, when Elsa's ice powers are revealed, he tries to turn the people of Arendelle against their queen.

Sorcery! I knew there was something dubious going on here.

Poor Anna discovers that the duke is a terrible dancer. He throws her around the dance floor at the royal ball.

Yzma

THE EMPEROR'S NEW GROOVE

Yzma has always been close to Emperor Kuzco. After all, she raised him. So when Kuzco fires her, Yzma cannot stand the rejection. She even tries to kill Kuzco with a magic potion, but she accidentally turns herself into a tiny kitten instead.

Long, spiderlike eyelashes

No hat is too big for her to wear

Brrrrilliant!

Sir Hiss

ROBIN HOOD

Sir Hiss is one slimy snake of a guy. He works for Prince John and tries to help him plot against Robin Hood. Like John, Sir Hiss loves to steal from the poor. His biggest problem is that Prince John doesn't always listen to him!

Red cap with white feather

I tried to tell you, sire, but, no, no, no, no. You wouldn't listen!

Olive-coloured scaly body

Sir Hiss likes to whisper secrets to Prince John by hissing in his ear.

25

Captain Hook

Beware the wickedest pirate who ever sailed the seven seas! Hook is nasty through and through. He plays all sorts of evil tricks to get what he wants. He kidnaps princesses, and he makes children walk the plank. He even shoots his own men for singing! Only Peter Pan can keep this menacing pirate in order.

About Captain Hook

- The thing he fears the most is the Croc that long ago ate his hand.
- He can speak the fairies' language and can understand Tinker Bell.
- He once sent a time bomb to Peter Pan disguised as a gift.

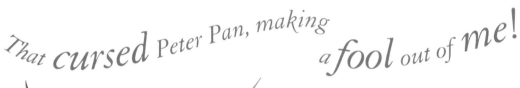

*That **cursed** Peter Pan, making a **fool** out of me!*

Peter Pan

The boy who never grew up is the real master of Never Land. Hero of the Lost Boys and adored by Tinker Bell, Peter Pan tries to protect everyone from Hook's wicked plots.

Captain Hook is ready to push Peter Pan off the top of the mast!

Ostrich-feathered hat

Hook in the place of his missing hand

Gold-trimmed dress coat

Soft-hearted Smee

While Captain Hook can behave in savage ways, he loves to be looked after. His right-hand man, Smee, is always ready with a cheery word or a fiendish plan for his "Cap'n".

Smee covers Captain Hook with a blankie when he gets a cold.

Flying foe

This one-handed pirate has one great wish – to rid the world of Peter Pan! Why? Because Pan fed the captain's left hand to a crocodile, forcing him to wear a hook.

Tick, tock, tick, tock... the crocodile that ate Hook's hand (and his clock!) is still after him.

27

The Jolly Roger

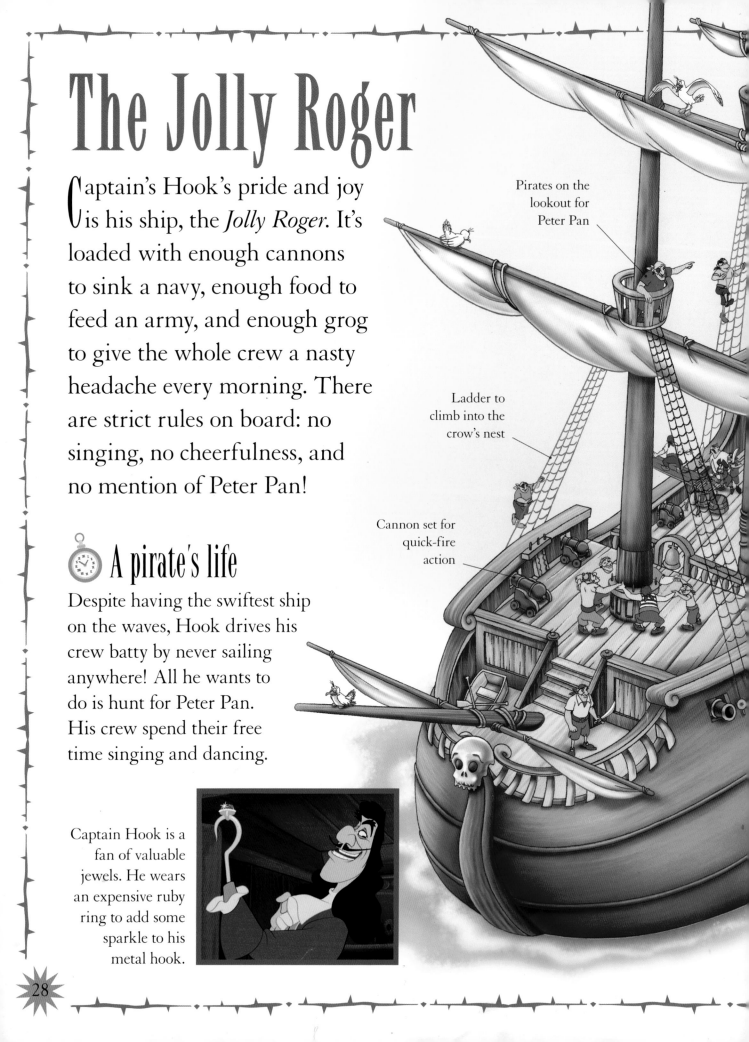

Captain's Hook's pride and joy is his ship, the *Jolly Roger*. It's loaded with enough cannons to sink a navy, enough food to feed an army, and enough grog to give the whole crew a nasty headache every morning. There are strict rules on board: no singing, no cheerfulness, and no mention of Peter Pan!

A pirate's life

Despite having the swiftest ship on the waves, Hook drives his crew batty by never sailing anywhere! All he wants to do is hunt for Peter Pan. His crew spend their free time singing and dancing.

Pirates on the lookout for Peter Pan

Ladder to climb into the crow's nest

Cannon set for quick-fire action

Captain Hook is a fan of valuable jewels. He wears an expensive ruby ring to add some sparkle to his metal hook.

Hook's luxurious cabin

The crew's filth-ridden quarters

Pirates share their beds with fleas and lice

Secret store of spare gunpowder, cutlasses, cannonballs, and rum

🕰 Cannibal Cove

The *Jolly Roger* often sits in Pirate's Cove, a sheltered harbour tucked near Never Land's island. Hook was last seen nearby, swimming for his life as he was chased by a hungry crocodile!

This sunny isle may look peaceful, but it is constantly overrun with pesky pirates.

🕰 Cruel Captain

Captain Hook is not only cruel to his enemies, but he is also vicious to his own pirates. The vain captain can fly into a temper tantrum easily, and he cheers up only when his pirates find him some treasure.

Captain Hook imprisons Tinker Bell so she cannot save Peter.

Hook's pirates love treasure. They don't mind whether they find it for themselves or steal it!

Deception

W hat lies beneath the surface of these selfish villains is never pretty. But some go to great lengths to hide their true dark sides. They can pretend to be a friend, a teacher, or even a parent. It's hard to know who you can trust!

Mother Gothel

TANGLED

Sly Mother Gothel is determined to have access to Rapunzel's magical hair, which keeps her looking young. In her crazed desperation, she kidnaps Rapunzel, locks her in a tower, and spends 18 years pretending to be her kind, but overprotective, mother.

Looks youthful, although she's several hundred years old

Elegant gold trim

Mother knows best!

Rapunzel grows up believing that Mother Gothel actually cares about her.

Give me the Mask, Hero.

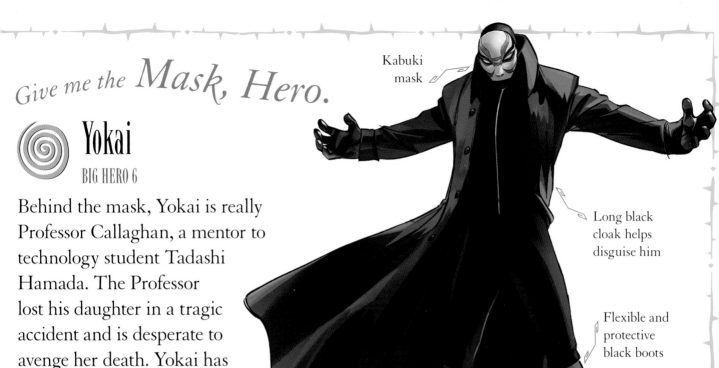

Kabuki mask

Long black cloak helps disguise him

Flexible and protective black boots

Yokai
BIG HERO 6

Behind the mask, Yokai is really Professor Callaghan, a mentor to technology student Tadashi Hamada. The Professor lost his daughter in a tragic accident and is desperate to avenge her death. Yokai has extraordinary powers, including the ability to control a massive army of microbots. His mission is destruction, and he seems unstoppable.

Kaa
THE JUNGLE BOOK

Kaa wants Mowgli to believe he has his best interests at heart. However, the snake is always hungry, and it looks like Mowgli is on the menu! Kaa's hypnotic eyes are his greatest power – he uses them to lure Mowgli into his coils.

Trussst in me.

Long neck wrapped into tight coils

Mowgli is hypnotised by Kaa's speech and his mesmerising eyes.

Gaston

With sweeping hair and an excellent physique, Gaston is the best-looking guy in the village. Women love him, and men want to be near him. But under those good looks, there is a vain and greedy man. Gaston thinks his muscles will impress everyone – even Belle. He couldn't be more wrong!

Self-assured

Gaston wants Belle to marry him, but he does not want her to read or to think for herself! Instead, he wants her to stay at home all day and mend his stinky socks! She is less than impressed by him.

Belle is not interested in this arrogant and selfish man. Who does he think he is?

Big and brawny

Gaston loves no one more than himself. With his handsome good looks and athletic prowess, he has lots of admirers – but Belle is not one of them.

Gaston loves to look at himself in the mirror. His best friend, LeFou, adores him, too.

About Gaston

- Gaston is the town hero.
- He is sure that he is better than everyone else. And he isn't afraid to tell them!
- He eats five dozen eggs for breakfast to keep himself big and strong.

Gaston has a handsome face… and he knows it!

Long hair tied in a ponytail

Extremely athletic build

Hunting boots

Brutal hunter

When Gaston doesn't get his way, he becomes vicious and cruel. In a jealous rage over Belle, he leads the villagers to hunt down the Beast and tries to kill him!

Gaston leads an angry mob of townspeople to attack the Beast in his castle.

It's *not right for* a *woman* to read.

33

Revenge

Some villains are driven to evil by moments from their pasts. It doesn't matter whether those moments built up over years or whether they were over in seconds. These villains' lives are transformed because they simply cannot let go of the past.

Dawn Bellwether

ZOOTOPIA

Assistant Mayor Bellwether may seem timid and mild-mannered, but under all of that fluffy wool, she's ruthless! This sheep is tired of not being taken seriously by her boss, the Mayor. She's willing to go to dangerous lengths to get her revenge.

Neat, woolly hairstyle

Fuzzy ankles with well-groomed hooves

Sensible clothing with a floaty skirt

I framed Lionheart. I can frame you, too!

It's almost impossible to believe sweet Dawn could behave badly.

Everyone would tell you to let it go and **move on,** *but don't!*

Signature black bowler hat

Well-worn (and torn) coat

High-heeled brown boots

Bowler Hat Guy
MEET THE ROBINSONS

As a kid, he was Mike "the Goob" Yagoobian, orphanage roommate of a boy named Lewis. After Lewis kept him up late one night working on an invention, the Goob missed a crucial catch in a baseball game. His shame grew into rage, and the Goob grew into the villainous Bowler Hat Guy.

Bowler Hat Guy is always trying to do something to ruin Lewis' life. He is set on revenge.

Evil Queen

Blood-red lipstick

Stiff, high-necked collar

Magic Mirror on the wall, who is the meanest queen of all? Snow White's wicked stepmother, that's who! She is obsessed with being "the most beautiful in the land". Unfortunately, as well as a queen, she's also a wicked witch with a laboratory full of potions to make sure no one surpasses her beauty.

Black cloak blends into the shadows

About the Evil Queen

- She is beautiful on the outside, but she has an evil heart.
- She has a pet raven who knows all her secrets.
- She makes Snow White dress in rags and work as a servant.

Royally mean

The Queen is jealous of her stepdaughter Snow White's beauty. She is driven even madder by Snow White's popularity, so she hatches a plan to get rid of her once and for all.

The Queen has a peacock carved into her throne. She thinks it reflects her beauty.

Evil magic

In a rage, the jealous Queen orders her faithful huntsman to cut out Snow White's heart. When that plan fails, she creates, and then drinks, a potion to change her own appearance in order to trick Snow White.

A potent potion transforms the Queen's appearance. The vain Queen thinks she looks like a kindly granny.

Red apple

Next, the Queen cooks up a poisoned apple. Whoever takes a bite will catch "the Sleeping Death" and appear to have died. Snow White is too trusting to suspect there is anything wrong.

Go on! Have a bite.

Hooded cloak and walking stick add to the disguise

Snow White does not recognise her stepmother in disguise. She believes the apple will make her dreams come true.

Wicked Ways

To her subjects, she is simply a proud, cold-hearted queen. Little do they suspect that under her throne room is a labyrinth of dark passages where she works her evil magic – a place of echoes and shadows that many have entered but few have escaped from. Creep in and take a look around – if you dare!

Magic Mirror

Every day, the Queen consults with the Magic Mirror hanging in her secret chamber. She demands the truth. Unfortunately, when she learns that she is not the most beautiful in the land, she is filled with rage.

When she stands before the mirror, it asks her, "What wouldst thou know, my Queen?"

The Queen keeps a book of evil spells in her dungeon.

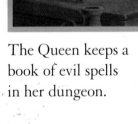

Raven

The closest thing the Queen has to a friend is her pet raven. The raven often sits on top of a skull in the secret dungeon. When things get too scary, he likes to climb inside to hide.

Secret staircase known only to the Queen (and rats)

Furious after discovering that Snow White is still alive, the Queen heads down into the dungeon to create the poisoned apple.

Pet raven likes to have a good view of the goings-on

Spell books

Skeleton scales for measuring out nasty ingredients

Frightening potions always being cooked up

Royally Spoiled

I'm now the most powerful virus in the arcade.

These kings, queens, and princes love being in charge and crave lots of attention. But if they don't get their way, they can get royally angry. When that happens, it's best to run for cover!

Mostly bald head with tufts of grey hair

Tidy, red bow tie

Only four fingers on each hand

King Candy
WRECK-IT RALPH

King Candy is the ruler of a kart-racing video game. He seems like a noble, sweet guy. He even lives in a sugar castle and hands out candy. The truth is, he is crazed and cruel and will do anything to stay in control of his gaming world.

Loves wearing royal robes

Mother always did like Richard best.

Prince John
ROBIN HOOD

Prince John is eager to sit on the throne while his brother Richard, the real king, is out of the country. This cowardly prince steals from the poor, so he can have more money for himself. He is also vain and weak, and he bullies everyone around him.

Queen of Hearts

ALICE IN WONDERLAND

The Queen of Hearts is the queen of temper tantrums, too. When she plays a simple game of croquet with Alice, she becomes furious when Alice starts to win. That's when the crazy queen threatens to chop off Alice's head!

Off with their heads!

Small gold crown perched on her head

Wide skirted red and black royal robes

Uses a flamingo as a croquet mallet

The card soldiers are the Queen of Hearts' loyal servants. They are terrified of her.

Scar

Disgruntled and deceitful, Scar is second in line to the throne and forever jealous of his brother, King Mufasa. When his nephew, Simba, is born, pushing him even further down the royal line, Scar is determined to make his way back to being the top cat of Pride Rock – whatever it takes.

About Scar

- Scar's weakness is telling lies. Eventually even his hyenas don't trust him.
- He is too jealous to attend the celebration of Simba's birth.
- He hates being told what to do.

Sinister slouch

Untamed black mane

Mean, jealous eyes

Twisted smile

Respect for the king-to-be

Simba, the cub who would be king, is Scar's biggest enemy. Mufasa knows this and orders Scar to treat Simba with respect. Naturally, the two-faced villain pretends to be Simba's best pal.

Scar mocks the younger lion by calling himself a "monkey's uncle".

Death plot

After Scar has the hyenas start a wildebeast stampede, Mufasa tries to save Simba. Sadly, the great king dies in the process, and young Simba is distraught.

Scar could not be happier to see his brother dead, but he lets Simba take the blame.

Scar's downfall

When the adult Simba returns to challenge Scar, the pride turn on their cowardly king. He admits that he killed Mufasa before delivering a final snack to the hyenas – himself!

I'm surrounded by **idiots.**

These heinous hyenas, Shenzi, Banzai, and Ed, are Scar's henchmen.

Too busy arguing to do much damage

The Pride Lands

E very land has its story, and the Pride Lands tell a tale of one vengeful lion and his low-down, mean, back-stabbing rise to power. Happily, they also tell the tale of Scar's fall and suitably gruesome end. It's all part of the idea that governs the land here, "the circle of life".

Tree of Life, with Rafiki, the wise baboon, meditating underneath

Simba escapes the hyenas by running through these thorns

Gorge wall where Mufasa saves Simba but is sent to his death by Scar

A shadowy place

Mufasa tells Simba that everything the light touches is the lions' kingdom. But on the northern border of the Pride Lands, there is a dark domain where elephant bones rot and dangerous characters lurk.

Naturally, this nasty neighbourhood is where Scar loves to hang out.

Pride Rock, home of Mufasa's family

Scar's cave

Water hole where the animals come to drink and bathe

Steep-sided gorge is a dangerous spot for lions

Hyena lair where Scar announces plans to be king

Elephant graveyard entrance

Devastated

After Scar takes over as king, the kingdom turns into a wasteland. His army of hyenas creates chaos, ruining the land and allowing the rest of the animals to starve.

Scar is such an evil and terrible leader that the Pride Lands are destroyed when he is king.

Forbidden area

Simba and his friend Nala are forbidden from going as far as this sinister place. The cubs don't listen and soon regret their actions when they are cornered by three hungry hyenas.

Simba and Nala are amazed to see the bones lying in the elephant graveyard.

The Power of Transformation

Trying to defend yourself against wicked characters is never easy. It gets even harder when the villains in question have the ability to change into something completely different. Not only is this terrifying, but it can be downright confusing, too!

A tip of the hat from
Dr Facilier!

Skull and crossbones on his top hat

Red waistband

 ## Dr Facilier

THE PRINCESS AND THE FROG

A voodoo sorcerer, Dr Facilier is always luring people into bad deals. He gives them whatever they say they want, even changing their appearances. But they end up much worse off than before. Known as the "Shadow Man", he spreads darkness wherever he goes.

Dr Facilier tricks Naveen, turning him into a frog.

Shabby mop of purple hair

*I'm the **magnificent**, marvellous, **mad** Madam Mim.*

She wants to destroy Arthur since he is good

Madam Mim
THE SWORD IN THE STONE

Madam Mim is an angry witch. She has powerful magic and can change herself into different creatures of all shapes and sizes. Sadly, she does not use her powers for good. Mim is never happier than when things are dreadful. She hates anything good – especially sunshine!

Chernabog
FANTASIA

This dark, horned villain starts out as a looming mountain peak and transforms into a monster. He has lots of magical powers, including his ability to grow. The good news is that the sun sends him back to his hiding place every day.

Chernabog stretches his wings and casts a shadow over a village far below.

Cruella De Vil

Cruella is a rich and spoiled aristocrat who is simply crazy about furs. She has violent mood swings and can be ruthless without any sign of guilt. Owning a Dalmatian fur coat is Cruella's dream, and she is prepared to steal poor little puppies to satisfy her evil desires.

I live for furs! I worship furs!

Unwanted guest

Anita went to school with Cruella. She and her husband, Roger, invite Cruella to meet their Dalmatians Pongo and Perdita, along with their 15 puppies. They soon discover that Cruella is pretty crazy!

Distinctive black and white hair

Pointed shoes match her spiky personality

Cruella is a terrifying sight at the door of Roger and Anita's home.

48

Cruel lady

Cruella mocks Roger and tries to intimidate him, but he refuses to back down! He wants to protect his wife and his dogs from her.

Roger refuses to let Cruella get away with his Dalmatian puppies.

 ## Crazy driver

Cruella drives an expensive red and black car, but she is a crazy driver! This reckless road hogger drives herself right off the road!

Cruella has had her car custom made to suit her own explosive character.

Favourite coat made from rare fox fur

About Cruella

⚡ She is obsessed with anything black and white.

⚡ She thinks everyone can be bought with a fat cheque.

⚡ Cruella hates waiting for anything. She's always in a rush.

 ## The Baduns

Horace and Jasper Badun work for Cruella. She hires them to steal the puppies. Later, they take the puppies to Cruella's creepy mansion to dogsit. Neither man is particularly bright. The dogs easily outwit them!

Cruella causes a piece of ceiling to fall on Horace

Hell Hall

After Horace and Jasper Badun kidnap the puppies, they take them to Cruella's dark and creepy mansion where they plan to keep them and later kill them! As Cruella would rather spend her cash on tasteless furry fashions than on the hall's upkeep, her ancestral home is falling apart at the seams.

Rotten old ruin

The fact that Hell Hall is such a ruin helps the kidnapped puppies make their escape. There are so many dark places to hide in and helpful holes to wriggle through.

Horace and Jasper look high and low for the lost puppies.

Lots of dogs

Horace and Jasper bring Pongo and Perdita's 15 puppies to Hell Hall, along with 84 other Dalmatian puppies, totalling 99! If you add in Pongo and Perdita, that makes 101 Dalmatians.

Pongo and Perdita's puppies watch their favourite show on television. It helps them forget that they are in a scary situation.

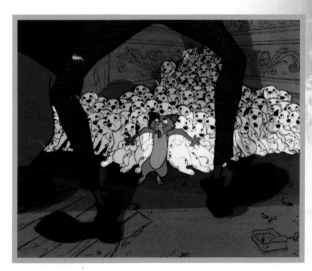

Sergeant Tibbs, the cat, tries to keep the puppies quiet and hidden from the Baduns.

Tall, smoking chimneys

Crumbling walls

Huge hole in the roof lets rain pour in

Damp walls covered in moss

Window frames riddled with woodworm

Filthy windows last cleaned in 1872

51

Filled with Greed

These greedy characters always want more. More diamonds, more money, and more objects that do not belong to them. They will steal and cheat to get them and will destroy anyone who tries to get in their way!

Wild, fiery hair

Fancy fur coat

Bianca wants to hide inside Medusa's suitcase.

I want that diamond!

Madame Medusa

THE RESCUERS

Madame Medusa loves her diamonds more than anything else in the world. She owns a pawn shop where she gathers as many diamonds as she can. Her greatest wish is to get her hands on the Devil's Eye, the largest diamond in the world.

Holds Maui's magical fishhook

Sparkly hoard stuck to his back

From treasures to junk, Tamatoa wears everything he collects on his 50-foot-wide back.

Tamatoa

MOANA

This show-off crab has a big ego and a lot of claws for grabbing things. He lives in Lalotai, the realm of the monsters, and he collects special objects from the sea. He is especially fond of shiny things because he can see his own reflection in them. His greatest wish is to own the heart of Te Fiti, the mother island.

Bill Sykes

OLIVER AND COMPANY

Sykes often sits in the shadows, with a mean smile and his vicious dogs. He is a big, greedy bully. He threatens his victims and always insists people owe him money. He doesn't seem to care about anything but himself and his big piles of cash.

Sykes loves to order people around

Doberman pinschers, Roscoe and DeSoto

This has all been very entertaining, but now the party is over.

53

Shere Khan

Shere Khan is the most feared animal in the jungle, but he has one great fear of his own – Man. He hates their fire and their weapons and will do anything to keep Man away from his home. He has made it his mission to destroy Mowgli the Man-cub. Even the big bear Baloo cannot keep Mowgli safe from the tiger's sharp claws.

Eavesdropping

Shere Khan hears that Mowgli is no longer being protected by the panther Bagheera. He sees this as his chance to track down the Man-cub and begins his ruthless hunt.

Shere Khan is a little impressed that Mowgli does not run away from him.

About Shere Khan

- Shere Khan means "Tiger King" in Persian and Hindi.
- Unlike other animals in the jungle, Shere Khan does not get hypnotised by the snake Kaa.
- Shere Khan's calm manner can be just as scary as his roar.

You're trying my patience.

Khan is usually calm but can be vicious

Powerful paws

 ## Friend in need

Mowgli has a secret weapon when it comes to fighting Shere Khan – friendship. Baloo is a big bear with a big heart. He puts his life on the line to save his friend Mowgli.

Baloo grabs Shere Khan's tail. As he struggles to break free, Mowgli has time to escape.

 ## Defeat

The fire Shere Khan fears is what helps Mowgli get the better of him in the end. The brave Man-cub returns to scare away Shere Khan by tying a burning branch to the tiger's tail.

Shere Khan has always feared fire. The sight of it alone is enough to send him into a panic.

Animals Unwelcome

While some villains depend on their animal sidekicks, these cunning characters think that they are much better than any pesky animal. They use every trick in the book to get one over their animal foes.

Edgar Balthazar
THE ARISTOCATS

Edgar is Madame Bonfamille's butler, and he was an honest and loyal one at first. However, that all changes when he learns that her cats – not he – will inherit his boss' entire fortune. Filled with greed and jealousy, he is determined to get rid of the cats.

Evil Edgar mixes sleeping pills with the cats' milk!

Butler's uniform

Cats inherit first, and I come after the cats?!

Berlioz, Marie, and Toulouse are Madame's pampered cats

Poacher's hat with crocodile teeth

Wears a bandana around his neck

Percival McLeach

THE RESCUERS DOWN UNDER

This cruel man likes to capture rare animals and sell them for their fur and feathers. He lies easily to make sure he gets what he wants. And he wants nothing more than to get his hands on the great golden eagle, Marahute.

He's even willing to kidnap and kill brave young Cody, who stands in the way of him finding his perfect prey.

You'll think *twice* before messing with *Percival McLeach!*

Vicious pet lizard Joanna

Prince Hans

Flushed, pink cheeks give the look of a man in love

As the youngest of 13 siblings, Prince Hans of the Southern Isles is not likely to inherit a kingdom of his own. His only chance to rule is by marrying into a different royal family. He sees an opportunity when he meets sweet, romantic Princess Anna of Arendelle. Hans will lie, cheat, and even kill to make his dream a reality.

You were SO desperate for love, you were willing to marry me just like that.

❄ Too good to be true?

At first, Hans seems like a nice guy. He romances Anna, and she falls head over heels for him. They dance at the ball, and he even proposes to her on their first date!

Traditional dress of the Southern Isles

She knows it's a little crazy, but Anna is sure she has met her match.

About Hans

- He is well educated and a smooth talker.
- Hans is a skilled sword fighter.
- His greatest wish is to be a king.

Dishonest

Prince Hans hatches a devious plot to marry Princess Anna and then murder Queen Elsa so that he can take over the kingdom. He is so good at fooling people, he almost gets away with it.

Hans wins over the people of Arendelle with his fake kindness.

False hunt

Hans leads a group of volunteers to find Elsa when she runs away. The tricky prince pretends to be doing good, but he really only cares about taking power from the queen.

The people of Arendelle trust the charming prince.

Heartless

Hans refuses to help Anna when her heart is freezing and she needs an "act of true love" to survive. Anna is healed by her love for her sister instead. And just in time!

Hans has no love for anyone but himself. He ruthlessly betrays both Anna and Elsa.

Loyal Sidekicks

Where would wicked villains be without their foolhardy followers? Always there to assist their masters in times of need or help them plot a nasty mission, these characters help make everything worse!

Dr Facilier's Shadow
THE PRINCESS AND THE FROG

Dr Facilier's shadow has a life and evil personality all of its own. It can move of its own will, and sometimes it takes a different shape to its owner. The shadow reflects the mood of its master, which is downright evil!

Mr Smee
PETER PAN

Smee is Captain Hook's first mate, cook, and trusted assistant. Although he tries to carry out his boss's evil plans, his kind-hearted nature often gets in the way.

Lucifer
CINDERELLA

Lady Tremaine's pampered old cat is treated better than Cinderella is! He is never happier than when he is causing trouble. He chases mice, teases the dog, and messes up all of Cinderella's hard work.

Card Soldiers
ALICE IN WONDERLAND

The Queen of Hearts is as mean to her army of Card Soldiers as she is to everyone else! Even still, they are easily bent and persuaded to do her worst bidding – including beheading anyone who upsets her!

Brutus and Nero
THE RESCUERS

Madame Medusa may be the true villain, but Brutus and Nero are not exactly the nicest crocodiles in the swamp. They are fiercely loyal to the evil woman until she pushes them a bit too far, and they try to eat her.

61

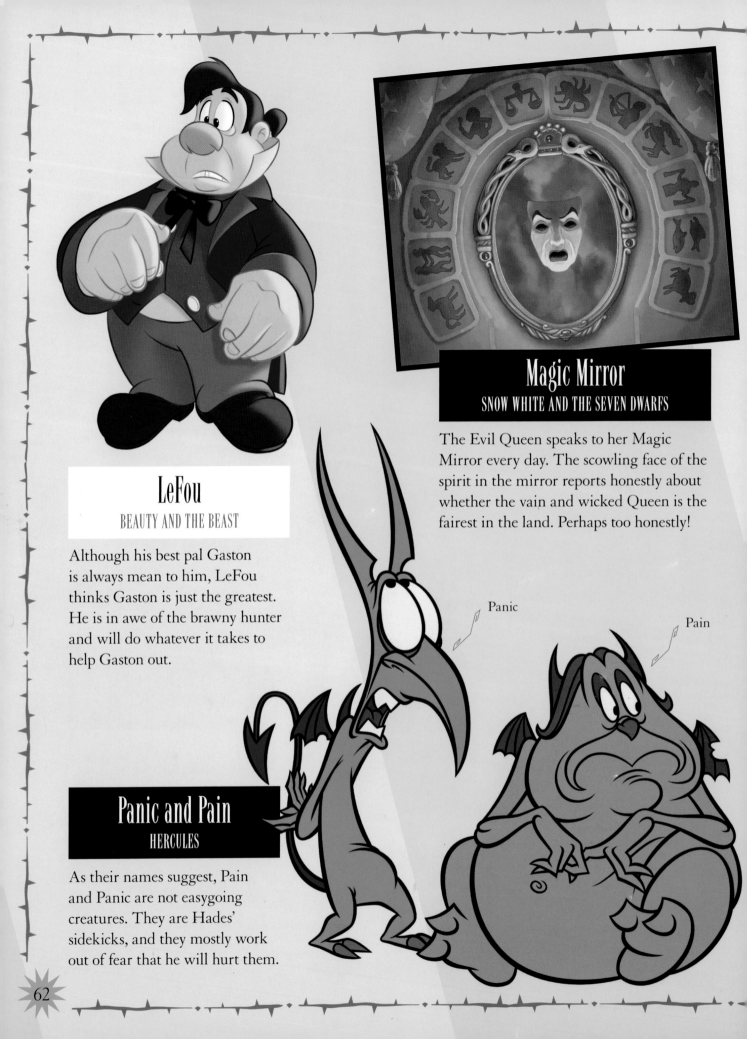

Magic Mirror
SNOW WHITE AND THE SEVEN DWARFS

The Evil Queen speaks to her Magic Mirror every day. The scowling face of the spirit in the mirror reports honestly about whether the vain and wicked Queen is the fairest in the land. Perhaps too honestly!

LeFou
BEAUTY AND THE BEAST

Although his best pal Gaston is always mean to him, LeFou thinks Gaston is just the greatest. He is in awe of the brawny hunter and will do whatever it takes to help Gaston out.

Panic

Pain

Panic and Pain
HERCULES

As their names suggest, Pain and Panic are not easygoing creatures. They are Hades' sidekicks, and they mostly work out of fear that he will hurt them.

Iago
ALADDIN

This wise-cracking parrot is a pal of the sorcerer Jafar. He is just as disgruntled and bitter as his boss. He also hates the Sultan, who won't stop stuffing crackers into his beak!

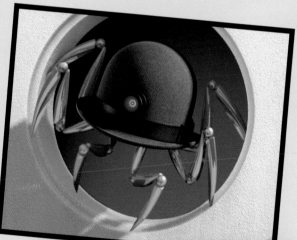

Doris
MEET THE ROBINSONS

DOR-15 (Doris) was originally invented as a helping hat. She should have assisted wearers in doing small tasks. However, she has an evil mind of her own. She teams up with Bowler Hat Guy, tricking him into thinking he is in charge!

Stabbington Brothers
TANGLED

These scary twin brothers have led a life of crime – but they have met their match in Mother Gothel. They help her find Rapunzel, but they soon learn that they shouldn't trust the double-crossing Gothel.

Emperor Zurg

Evil Emperor Zurg comes from the planet Xrghthung. He is the enemy of the Galactic Alliance, and he is pure evil! His main goal is to destroy the entire galaxy, and the greatest obstacle to his success is the good and noble space ranger Buzz Lightyear.

Eyes glow when he's angry

"Z" chestplate

Zurg world

Zurg has a big problem with being a "toy". He has that in common with his archenemy Buzz. When he is accidentally freed from his box at Al's Toy Barn, it doesn't take him long to catch up with Buzz.

Blaster shoots ion pellets

The evil Zurg is monitoring Buzz Lightyear's every move.

About Zurg

- He is the sworn destroyer of the Galactic Alliance.
- He keeps spare ion pellets in a special ammo pack in his cape.
- He is in total denial that he is a toy.

Surrender, Buzz Lightyear!
I have won!

⚡ Blaster battle

Buzz and Emperor Zurg face off in an epic battle. It's Buzz's blinking laser light against Zurg's rotating ion blaster!

Robotic armour hands

Emperor Zurg has the potential to destroy the universe. He must be stopped!

⚡ What a shock

Buzz Lightyear believes that Zurg killed his father. He is shocked beyond belief when the Emperor hits him with the truth: Zurg himself is actually the space ranger's father!

Almost invincible armour

Zurg decides to abandon world domination and focus on being a good dad instead!

Toy Enemies

It's tough to be a toy. It seems like there's danger lurking everywhere you turn. Poor plastic soldiers retreat, toy aliens make a quick exit, and dolls dash for cover as they try to escape from dogs, cats, kids, and even other nasty toys.

Let's go home and play!

Short, spiky haircut

Sid
TOY STORY

Toys tremble when they see this kid coming! Sid loves to torture toys – his freaky idea of playtime involves a brand-new doll, a surgical mask, and maybe a firecracker. His neighbour Andy's toys are terrified of him. He nearly blasts Buzz Lightyear to bits with a rocket!

Scud

TOY STORY

Sid's dog, Scud, aims to be every bit as destructive as the missile he is named after. The horrible hound likes tearing toys apart as much as his master does. With his determined and suspicious nature, he will chase down anything he can chew.

You keep forcing me to take **extreme** *measures.*

The Prospector

TOY STORY 2

Not a popular toy, the gold-digging Prospector has never been taken out of his box. He wants to retire to a museum where he will stay clean and spiffy. He acts like a kindly, grandfatherly figure to the other toys, but he's really a low-down sneak.

Dragon the cat

TOY STORY 4

Dragon is a cruel cat who strolls around an antiques store looking for stray toys. When he finds them, he's more than eager to destroy them. He is fast and fierce, and the toys live in fear of him finding them and tearing them apart!

Lotso

Lots-o'-Huggin' Bear, or Lotso for short, is a soft, plush, smiling teddy who lives at Sunnyside Daycare. He welcomes the new toys that arrive there with open arms… but he is not all he seems. Underneath his cuddly fur, Lotso is a bitter bear who takes his bad feelings out on other toys.

Abandoned

Lotso was once a good toy and friend, but then he was left at a rest stop with some other toys by their owner, Daisy. Since then, Lotso has been determined to control his own destiny.

Tough teddy

Lotso now lives at Sunnyside Daycare, where he rules over the other toys. He makes sure that they never step out of line. When Andy's toys arrive, they soon work out what Lotso is really like.

When Buzz refuses to join Lotso's gang of toy thugs, the bear has Buzz's factory settings reset.

Well, hello there! I'm Lots-o'-Huggin' Bear.

Lotso was heartbroken by his owner, Daisy, abandoning him on the roadside.

 # Dump fate

After behaving badly and treating his fellow toys cruelly, Lotso finally gets his comeuppance. A waste collector finds him and straps him to the grille of his truck!

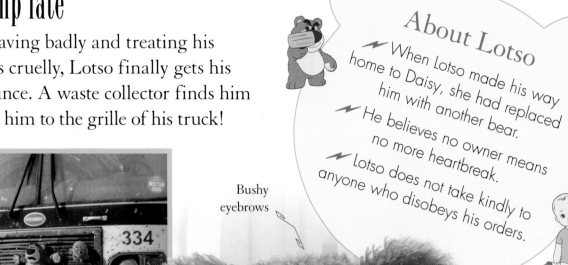

A muddy and bug-splattered frog teaches Lotso the rules of the road.

About Lotso

⚡ When Lotso made his way home to Daisy, she had replaced him with another bear.

⚡ He believes no owner means no more heartbreak.

⚡ Lotso does not take kindly to anyone who disobeys his orders.

Bushy eyebrows

Velvety, soft nose

Uses a walking stick

Lotso's Gang

New toys can hardly believe their luck when they arrive at Sunnyside Daycare. It is bright, colourful, and filled with children playing. But all is not as sunny as it seems at Sunnyside. In fact, there's a very dark side lurking beneath the surface.

Lotso believes that toys have to pay their dues and stick to the rules!

Sunnyside Daycare

No toy leaves Sunnyside – not if Lotso can help it! The bear and his gang of henchmen patrol the corridors of Sunnyside day and night to make sure that no toy escapes.

Bright colours make Sunnyside seem more fun than it really is.

Terrifying toys

Lotso is in charge of the toys at Sunnyside, but he has a team of terrifying henchmen to do his bidding. Even this motley bunch live in fear of their terrible leader.

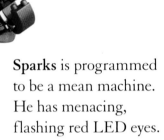

Ken works for Lotso in secret. He runs his creepy casino inside a vending machine.

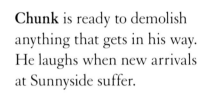

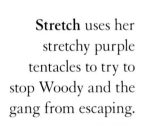

Sparks is programmed to be a mean machine. He has menacing, flashing red LED eyes.

Chunk is ready to demolish anything that gets in his way. He laughs when new arrivals at Sunnyside suffer.

Stretch uses her stretchy purple tentacles to try to stop Woody and the gang from escaping.

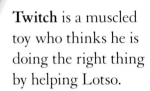

Twitch is a muscled toy who thinks he is doing the right thing by helping Lotso.

Big Baby is well worn, with a broken eye, a dirty onesie, and a reluctance to trust anyone but Lotso.

71

Syndrome

As a kid, Buddy Pine worshipped Mr Incredible and wanted to be his sidekick. After Mr Incredible rejected his help, Buddy reinvented himself as the evil Syndrome and went from his number-one fan to his number-one enemy. Now his sole mission is revenge and to destroy every Super he can.

Incrediboy

Buddy used to call himself "Incrediboy", but he was really just a super bother to Mr Incredible. He was an incredible nuisance, distracting him on a serious mission.

To get back at his enemy, Mr Incredible, Syndrome wants to prove how clever and powerful he is.

Evil inventions

Syndrome may not have special powers, but he is an evil genius. He has spent many years developing dangerous and terrifying gadgets.

Syndrome's secret weapon is the Omnidroid – an intelligent robot that can recreate any super power.

About Syndrome

⚡ He lives in (and terrorises!) the city of Metroville.

⚡ Syndrome has invented a suit that allows him to fly.

⚡ He has waited 15 years to get his revenge against Mr Incredible.

I'll be a bigger hero than you ever were.

Red hair resembles an angry flame

Eye mask hides his true identity

Giant "S" on his suit

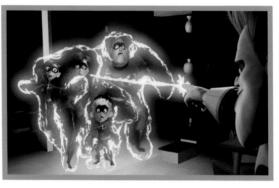 **Energy force field**

Using his utility gauntlets, Syndrome can fire energy blasts from his fingers. This freezes his victims to the spot. They can't move or even speak!

The Incredibles family falls victim to Syndrome's zero point energy technology.

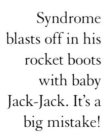 **Kidnapping**

After his plans are foiled, Syndrome grabs Jack-Jack Incredible. He plans to raise him as his evil sidekick. But Jack-Jack is one baby who is not going bye-bye without a fight!

Syndrome blasts off in his rocket boots with baby Jack-Jack. It's a big mistake!

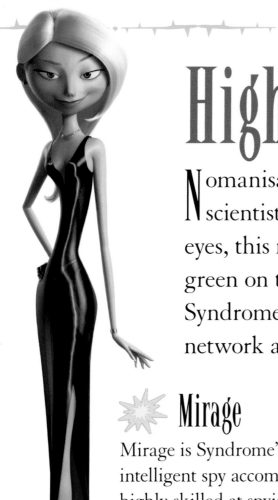

High-tech Hideaway

Nomanisan Island is the perfect base for a mad scientist to create evil inventions. Far from prying eyes, this mysterious volcanic island looks lush and green on the outside. Under its surface, however, Syndrome has developed the ultimate high-tech network as his headquarters.

 ## Mirage

Mirage is Syndrome's cool and intelligent spy accomplice. She is highly skilled at spying. Eventually, she turns against Syndrome and helps the Supers escape.

Mirage acts like the perfect hostess. She easily hides her secret identity from Mr Incredible.

Nomanisan Island

Syndrome's compound is built inside and around a smoking volcano. It also features boiling lava beds and plunging waterfalls. He clearly likes living dangerously!

The island is covered with lush greenery

Velocipods

Syndrome's thugs fly silver, disc-shaped velocipods around the island. They are kept in the air by sharp spinning blades, can change direction easily, and fly at extremely high speeds.

Syndrome's guards use Velocipods to try to chase down and capture Violet and Dash Incredible.

Hacking network

Syndrome has a massive computer network. It allows him to spy on his enemies from a safe distance. It also controls most of the headquarters and its mechanical devices.

Syndrome's powerful computer system helps him in his mission to destroy Supers.

 Super demise

Volcano at the centre of Nomanisan Island

Syndrome's plot fails miserably, and he ends up getting his cape caught in his own jet's engines. Sometimes evil inventors can be too clever for their own good!

Syndrome is destroyed by his own low-tech cape.

Evelyn Deavor

This bitter and angry genius inventor blames the Supers for not saving her father's life. Since he died, Evelyn Deavor has built a massive tech empire with her brother. She works her wicked ways to destroy Supers and create havoc in the world. While Evelyn seems calm on the outside, she is filled with rage.

Shirt with fashionable black and white print

 ## Double trouble

Evelyn and her brother, Winston, inherited their father's company, DevTech. They have built the company into the biggest electronics firm in the world. Winston loves Supers, while Evelyn… not so much!

Casual work clothes

Evelyn loves her brother, but she doesn't always agree with him.

About Evelyn

⚡ She believes that Supers cause more harm than good.

⚡ She is a genius in the tech world. Even as a child, she was able to solve extremely difficult problems.

⚡ She gets really upset if her pizza is delivered late and cold.

 ## Not so chill

Evelyn is so friendly to the Supers that she quickly earns their trust. They open up to her with absolutely no idea what this ruthless villain is really capable of.

Evelyn seems eager to help the Supers using her incredible intelligence and tech skills.

 ## Screenslaver

Evelyn uses Hypno-goggles to control people. Their hypnotic screens turn a pizza boy into her "Screenslaver" puppet. She also gets the goggles onto the Supers to make them look bad in front of the world.

Evelyn watches as her Super victims act under her evil command. She wants everyone to hate them.

The fact that you saved me doesn't make you right.

Unmasked

Even after Evelyn reveals herself to be the Screenslaver, Elastigirl still saves her life. An ungrateful Deavor refuses to admit she was wrong, despite being hauled off by the police!

Kind-hearted Elastigirl makes sure Evelyn is brought back to the ground safely.

Terrible Scarers

While lots of monsters try to collect scare energy from kids, these two cross a line when they kidnap a child. Randall wants to be the top Scarer, while Waternoose is motivated by greed. Together, they make a truly terrible team.

Brave Boo overcomes her fears when she is captured by Randall. She pulls on his antennae and hits him with a baseball bat.

Gimme that kid!

Creepy expression

Can change colour to camouflage

Randall
MONSTERS, INC.

Frightening kids was a good honest job until Randall came along and cheated his way into top spot at Monsters, Inc. It isn't long before two of the organisation's employees, Mike and Sulley, discover his secret, and this lousy lizard ends up at the wrong end of a shovel!

Eight legs can cause plenty of mischief

Kids these days. They just don't **get scared** *like they used to.*

Smart tuxedo
jacket

Seven fingers
on each hand

Sharp,
crablike legs

Henry J. Waternoose

MONSTERS, INC.

Monsters, Inc., collects scream energy to power
Monstropolis. As head of the company,
Waternoose gets desperate when it collects fewer
screams and makes less money. Underneath his
professional appearance, he is dishonest and
devious. He's quick to betray his friends for profit.

Waternoose is a tough boss. He wants
only the best monsters to become
Scarers. This will help keep
Monsters, Inc., alive.

Charles F. Muntz

In the 1930s Charles F. Muntz was a beloved adventurer and explorer. Fans went crazy for news of his latest exploits in his *Spirit of Adventure* airship. He was a hero to people around the world. However, one ill-fated trip to Paradise Falls caused his career to nose-dive.

About Charles F. Muntz

⚡ His trips to exotic locations used to make the news regularly.

⚡ He spent 70 years trying to capture another giant bird.

⚡ His pack of attack dogs are always on the lookout for unwanted guests.

13-foot -tall bird

Eats chocolate, balloons, and walking canes

Charles claimed he had found the skeleton of a giant coloured bird in Paradise Falls.

🌐 Fall of a hero

No one believes Charles when he claims to have found a giant bird. As a result, his membership of the National Explorers Society is removed. Humiliated and bitter, he lives the next 70 years as a recluse, desperate to restore his reputation.

Charles is determined to find the bird and prove he was right!

Adventure is out there!

Cold, green eyes

Brown leather jacket from his youth

Walking cane… or weapon

Suspicious

Charles lives in a cave with his pack of dogs. After years without seeing people, chatting to his dogs is all the conversation he gets. He has become very wary of strangers.

Charles' dogs wear special collars that allow them to speak to him.

Long wait

His search for the mysterious bird has led him to ruthless acts. He'll stop at nothing to find his prize. That includes trying to destroy anyone who gets in his way.

Charles' search for the bird has become an obsession, turning him into a heartless man.

Chef Skinner

This is one sneaky chef! Skinner is a maniacal man who wants complete control over Gusteau's restaurant. He is short-tempered and treats everyone with cruelty and disrespect. He is also quite snobby about cooking, though Linguini proves to be a far better chef – which makes Skinner murderously jealous.

Welcome to hell!

Big attitude

He may be small, but this chef has big plans! He lets the restaurant run itself while he cooks up get-rich-quick schemes. His long-term plan is to inherit the restaurant.

Chef's hat is starched to stand as tall as possible

Arms folded in aggressive stance

A stepladder is a vital tool for this vertically challenged snooper.

82

About Chef Skinner

- Skinner is set to inherit Gusteau's restaurant if an heir is not found.
- He would do anything for money or power.
- He likes setting rat traps.

In the kitchen

Skinner is a greedy, bullying boss. The screaming tyrant keeps his kitchen in order – no one dares to criticise him. But he makes the atmosphere like a steaming battle zone.

The workers in the kitchen know it's best to avoid eye contact with Chef Skinner.

Dirty trick

Skinner discovers that Linguini is Gusteau's son. This means Linguini will inherit the restaurant instead of him! Enraged, Skinner tries to hide the truth until it is too late.

A DNA test on a strand of Linguini's hair proves that he is Gusteau's son.

Shocking truth

The mean chef is determined to find the secret of Linguini's cooking success. He's not prepared for the truth – that a talented rat named Remy has been hiding in Linguini's hat!

Skinner can hardly believe his eyes! He does not approve of rats in his kitchen!

Rat Remy is the real culinary genius

Careless Cars

These cars could not care less. That's mostly because they care only about themselves. Nasty down to their axles, these cars will stop at nothing to win on the track or off it. They don't care a jot about risking the lives of other cars.

Chick Hicks

CARS

Chick Hicks always seems to be the runner-up in the Piston Cup. Dislikable and downright desperate for that trophy, his only fan is himself. This veteran racer cheats and plays dirty tricks, but he would go much faster without those chips on his shoulder!

I'm not coming in behind you again, old man!

Stickers from sponsors

Chick Hicks is always nudging and knocking his opponents.

Clip-on moustache grill

Green paint matches "green" views

Wire coils in wheels connect to electric battery

Miles Axlerod

CARS 2

Miles Axlerod is rich and seems to be using his wealth to make the world a better place. But he's no environmental hero – the only green thing about him is his paint work! He is behind a plot to destroy race cars. He creates a fuel that makes racers explode!

Professor Z

CARS 2

Professor Z is a tiny car with a truly twisted mind. He designs dangerous weapons and relies on an army of loyal Lemon cars to carry out his cowardly plans. His most dangerous invention is a deadly electromagnetic radiation ray, which is a threat to every single car on the planet.

Why didn't my death ray kill you?

Wears a monocle

Ernesto de la Cruz

Ernesto de la Cruz was once the most popular and famous musician in the land. However, young Miguel learns that Ernesto was in actual fact a selfish and greedy man. The star killed his best friend, Miguel's great-great grandfather, all because he wanted to be rich and famous.

Héctor

Miguels' great-great grandfather, Héctor, had quit touring with Ernesto because he missed his family. Ernesto was so furious with his former double-act partner that he poisoned Héctor and stole his songs.

Héctor left his friend and the limelight to return to his family. Something Ernesto could not forgive.

Land of the Dead

De la Cruz now exists in the Land of the Dead. Even there he lives a life that is as extravagant as it was when he was alive. His enormous mansion is a symbol of his success.

De la Cruz's home attracts all the A-listers of the afterlife. It is the ultimate party destination.

About Ernesto

- Ernesto started out as a nobody from the little town of Santa Cecilia.
- He lied about performing all his own stunts in his movies.
- Hundreds of fans flock to see a statue of him in his hometown.

Performs wearing traditional sombrero

Legendary guitar

I am the one who is willing to do what it takes to seize my moment!

Singing star

Ernesto is used to performing for his devoted fans. He sings songs with powerful and inspiring messages, including one about seizing the chance to change your life. But he took his own message too seriously – deadly seriously, in fact!

In the afterlife, de la Cruz wears an all-white suit

Ernesto's audience turns against him when they realise what he is capable of.

87

Monstrous Creatures

Cruel creepy crawlies and beasts big and small are among the vilest villains around. Whatever their species or size, they have far greater strength than their foes. You can be sure that none of these creatures is man's best friend!

Mor'du
BRAVE

Once a vain and arrogant prince, Mor'du is now a bloodthirsty bear under a terrible spell. Standing over 13 feet tall, he is savage and fiercely strong. Everyone in the kingdom fears bears, but the deadly Mor'du is the most terrifying of all.

Glossy, black fur

Razer-sharp claws

Princess Merida is no match for Mor'du. He has the strength of 10 men.

It's a **bug-eat-bug** *world out there, Princess.*

Hopper
A BUG'S LIFE

The insect world never produced a greedier gangster than Hopper. The vicious leader of the grasshopper gang believes ants exist only to collect food for the grasshoppers. He threatens the ants and steals their food every year. Any resistance will be instantly squished – or so he thinks!

Intimidating stare

You think you can mess with me?

Large head crest

Wide wingspan for gliding

Thunderclap
THE GOOD DINOSAUR

Terrifying pterodactyl Thunderclap leads a gang of winged scavengers. The pterodactyls follow storms because it's easier to attack innocent animals afterward. They swoop down and gobble up wounded critters, with no mercy for their injured prey.

Thunderclap captures Spot after a thunderstorm. He nearly eats him!

Auto

In the year 2805, all humans have been evacuated from Earth and are living in luxury spaceships, like the *Axiom*. The *Axiom* is mostly run by a robotic autopilot named Auto. Over time, Auto develops an evil personality and does every wicked thing it can to prevent the ship and everyone on it from returning to Earth.

Designed to last 700 years in space

Piercing red, laser "eye"

Steering wheel shape

Sir, orders are: **Do not** *return to Earth*.

☢ In charge

A powerful corporation called Buy-n-Large is in charge of all aspects of life on Earth. It is behind a secret directive (code name AII3) given to all autopilots never to return to Earth.

The Captain has been happy to leave the running of the ship to Auto. He is used to taking it easy.

☢ WALL-E

Robotic waste collection unit WALL-E finds a plant on Earth. This proves that there is the potential for life on Earth – something Auto does not want anyone to find out.

When WALL-E won't give up the plant, Auto zaps him with a taser.

☢ Auto unarmed

As autopilot for the *Axiom*, Auto is in charge of the entire ship. He can control almost anything unless – and until – the humans wake up and start doing things on their own.

When the Captain realises that Auto is evil, he defeats the robot by simply turning it off.

About Auto

⚡ The only way to stop Auto is by shutting off its power.

⚡ Auto tries to destroy WALL-E, but love triumphs when visitor probe EVE saves her robot friend.

How Well Do You Know the Villains and Rivals?

Now that you have read all about the dreadful deeds of the villains, take this quiz to see how well you really know each one!

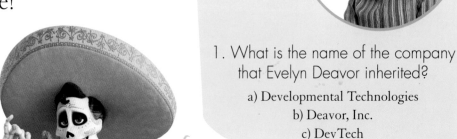

1. What is the name of the company that Evelyn Deavor inherited?

    a) Developmental Technologies
      b) Deavor, Inc.
        c) DevTech

2. Did Ernesto de la Cruz perform all his own stunts?

    a) Yes, of course!
b) No, he lied about that.
c) No, but he was honest with his fans about it.

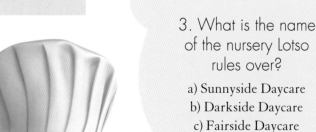

3. What is the name of the nursery Lotso rules over?

    a) Sunnyside Daycare
    b) Darkside Daycare
    c) Fairside Daycare

4. Who is the secret cooking star in Chef Skinner's kitchen?

    a) A mouse named Manny
    b) A rat named Remy
    c) A princess named Penny

5. Auto is the robotic autopilot on which ship?

    a) *Waxiom*
    b) *Pantheon*
    c) *Axiom*

6. Ursula disguises herself as which temptress?

a) Vanessa
b) Violet
c) Veronica

7. Who does Shere Khan want to destroy?

a) Bagheera
b) Baloo
c) Mowgli

9. How many older brothers does Hans have?

a) Fifteen
b) Twelve
c) Four

8. What is Jafar's official title?

a) Royal Pain
b) Royal Vizier
c) Sorcerer of Agrabah

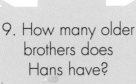

10. What does the Evil Queen want most in the world?

a) To be the most beautiful
b) To be the richest
c) To be the happiest

11. What is the name of Cruella's run-down home?

a) Monster Mansion
b) Hell Hall
c) Hovel House

12. He wants to track down Peter Pan, but which character makes Hook run in fear?

a) Wendy
b) Smee
c) The Croc

Answers: 1c 2b 3a 4b 5c 6a 7c 8b 9b 10a 11b 12c

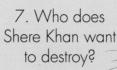